Selected Dreams from the Animal Kingdom

Selected Dreams from the Animal Kingdom

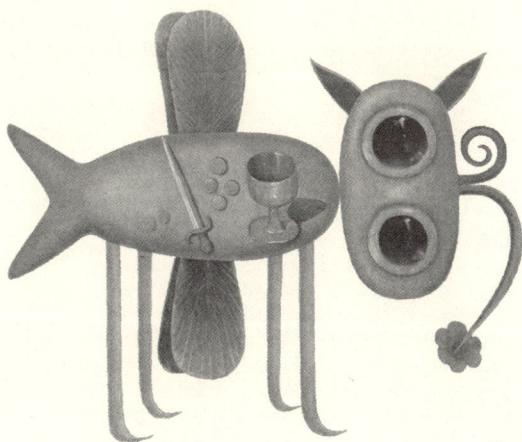

Poems by Judith Taylor

Zoo Press

Zoo Press • P.O. Box 22990 • Lincoln, Nebraska 68542
Printed in the United States of America

Distributed to the trade by The University of Nebraska Press
Lincoln, Nebraska 68588 • www.nebraskapress.unl.edu

Cover design by Merriam Massey © 2003

Cover painting, *The Surrealist* (*Le Surréaliste*), by Victor Brauner, 1947 © Victor Brauner, courtesy of the Peggy Guggenheim Collection, Venice

Library of Congress Cataloging-in-Publication Data

Taylor, Judith
  Selected dreams from the animal kingdom : poems / Judith
Taylor.– 1st ed.
    p. cm.
  ISBN 1-932023-05-4 (alk. paper)
  I. Title.
  PS3570.A94156 S45 2003
  811'.54–dc21

                                        2002155589

zoo014

First Edition

Acknowledgments

Grateful acknowledgment to the editors of the following publications in which these poems first appeared, sometimes in different versions:

88: "The Court Jester"; *Comstock Review*: "Aging Trip"; *Conduit*: "Mood Sonnet #3," "Mood Sonnet #5"; *Crab Orchard Review*: "Legacy"; *Crazyhorse*: "Tale"; *Ellipsis*: "Mood Sonnet #15"; *Fence*: "Mood Sonnet #8"; *Green Mountains Review*: "Big Mouth"; *The Journal*: "Mood Sonnet #20"; *Poetry*: "Persephone"; *Prairie Schooner*: "La Catrina," "Mood Sonnet #2," "Mood Sonnet #4," "Mood Sonnet #6," "Mood Sonnet #9," "Mood Sonnet #10," "Practicing," "The Secret Life of a Cloud"; *Quarterly West*: "Age of Ice," "Mood Sonnet #1," "Pumpkin Moon"; *Rivendell*: "How Am I Driving?"; *Runes*: "Mood Sonnet #16"; *Seneca Review*: "Mood Sonnet #13"; *Solo*: "Signal for the Eerie Light," "Tears"; *Sonora Review*: "Love in the Tenth Century"; *Spoon River Poetry Review*: "Accoutréments," 'Corroborating Evidence," "Euphoria," "Mood Sonnet #7," "Mood Sonnet #11," "Mood Sonnet #12," "Mood Sonnet #17," "Mood Sonnet #19," "The Mystery of Teeth," "A Tale of a Tutu" (Illinois Poet Feature, 2002); *Witness*: "River Barge," "Selected Dreams from the Animal Kingdom".

"Famous Pairs" appeared in *Ravishing DisUnities: Real Ghazals in English*, ed. Agha Shahid Ali, Wesleyan University Press, Published by University Press of New England, 2000.

"Burning," "Famous Pairs," "Love in the Tenth Century," "Persephone," "Tears," appeared in *Burning*, Portlandia Press, 1999.

Many friends have been helpful to me while I was writing these poems. I offer my deep thanks to Cal Bedient, Molly Bendall, Lin Benedek, Katherine Coles, Cathy Colman, Janet Kaplan, Patty Seyburn, David St.John, and Charles Harper Webb.

My gratitude to the Djerassi Resident Artists Program, The MacDowell Colony, the Ucross Foundation Residency Program, and the Virginia Center for the Creative Arts for their generous support.

To the memory of my mother and father

Table of Contents

I

II

I

This isn't piano, this is dreaming

—Duke Ellington

That spring night I spent
Pillowed on your arm
Never really happened
Except in a dream.
Unfortunately I am
Talked about anyway.

—Lady Suo

Pumpkin Moon

There are good reasons why we dream at night.
One's to keep us from being smug as we walk
around in sunlight wearing clothes and eating
foods that are good for you. I've been wearing
too much blue, I know. By day we wander
daubing our fears with iodine. If by day
hollowly the pines whistle, at night they're
seducers, lulling you to strange waywardness.
My dream was not uncommon: one kissed
surprising people and hid from friends. There
was a crass bit about a donkey that I'm not going
to tell but I am going to say that my ex-lover
sneaks into my sleep wherein he is either very fat
or quite small, neither of which he is in daylight.
Despite his size, we made out in his parent's van,
performed a buck-and-wing at a christening
and took to swinging from willows with the other
monkeys. Dear reader, do you want to decode
your dreams? I don't. O wide-awake person,
I know at night you ride the skies like I do,
hooting at the moon then wake up, a sense
of something gone. Night pines weave branches
into each other like enchanter's tales. The dark
road goes to places I don't know yet. I've just
arrived. Which way to the town, to the pond?
Adultery's not different from fairyland, or dream.
You must believe not what's real, but what's true.
My lover and I, people of the pumpkin moon,
inebriated on imagination. It is our joy. And
maybe it's easy to remain up there, skyward,
if you're the married one. I wouldn't know.
Reader, we're talking about love, so of course

some mornings I miss the tiny man fiercely.
I dutifully brush my teeth and scrub the strange
familiar lamenting night off my shiny face.

Tale

The hunters' guns pop, resound down the hills.
I'm wearing a knitted orange cap so they won't
hurt me. In Wyoming, they shoot first, then

ask if you're a deer. Today one came close
to the house, shook its adorable cloud butt. I'd
like to knit small tangerine snoods for the deer.

Not that I can knit, no, but the princess who knitted
twelve magic vests for her twelve brothers-turned-
into-swans certainly could. I can't recall why

they merited this cruel enchantment, some
sorceress was angry for something they did?
Being hunters, they deserved their fate?

This princess, who was not transformed herself,
spent all her days and nights knitting shirts
from nettles (which hurt a lot) for her twelve

swan-brothers. It was part of the magic deal --
blood from her dainty hands woven into the shirts.
She finished all in time but the twelfth, so

her youngest (and nicest) brother walks around
the castle with a large white wing. She did her best.
Once, a swan glided glamorously toward me and

a man to whom I wasn't married. The moon was full
of itself, male. When I reached out to touch it,
the swan snapped at my hand so we went back

to my room from whence not too much trouble ensued,
   but some. As I child I thought: Why should she
pay for her brothers' lives with torment? I would

be different. I wouldn't inflict pain, either. Ah, well.
   Whatever happened to us, whatever hurt home held,
wasn't physical. Mother lived life like a queen,

and she bore Father's gibes with a saintly carriage.
   She taught me that most situations can be endured
with a calm demeanor and the right outfit. One

of her credos: nice women always wear gloves.
   That way no one sees the blood, but it still hurts us,
mother, doesn't it?

Corroborating Evidence

When I woke up this morning my dream
wanted me to witness it. Don't strip me off
with your nightshirt, it said, don't try to fob

yourself off as a creature of the day. The dream
knows. The usual ballet of ablutions (splash)
and stretchings (ouch). I'm not going to be fooled

into climbing the stairway to memoir. Be pushed
off the banister, noiring all the way down.
Sorry. Sorrow trails some women like a small

yapping dog, like a favor someone else needs.
I refuse to adopt that cur. If we're going to put
on a play, I want to be Macbeth, not his Lady.

Primo, I've memorized Tomorrow and Tomorrow
having suffered through the kids' version
sans gore sans sex sans everything. Secunda,

I want to play the prime mover, history's acrobat.
On TV last night a cop, coerced by his chief,
covered up evidence of a crime. His strain,

defeat, his palpable guilt reflected how some of us
feel about certain scenes in our lives. I was
relieved the lead cop forgave him utterly.

My scream stopped sleep and I lay in my sweat
until morning. If at times I feel I'm drowning
in the Pacific of regret, my legs kick up

to the surface without my will. I'm a trained
swimmer. You wake yourself up from the unbearable.
You backstroke, you butterfly, you crawl.

Mood Sonnet # 1

Last night when the spider wrote its stupid sentence, you awoke.
"You've failed again to be humorous in your own cosmos."
The hours' hooves reflecting dark in pearled rainpools.
Mother was there, her exquisite, inappropriate ornaments.
Christmas five months away, but the guests smiled, white teeth.
You were eating strange food again, tamarinded, saffroned.
The white dawns opal and oppressive as it milks away.
You know how the restless breaks of your composure leak ink.
How these failed approaches orphan into weathering zones.
What the calendar stitches familiar to you as your aging body.
Real are the horses, suddenly red-brown in the fog's relenting.
Possibly the dew on the spider's web, but the glint of stories seduces.
Into the shell of dreaming disappear with your hoodoo mascara.
Don't forget to nail all blessing messages to the solid wall.

Mood Sonnet #2

The path is distraction, polkaing off in wavy directions.
Yet you are immobile sitting at a computer wearing green.
Thinking about fairy tales, the heroines and their fates.
Thin hands' branching veins, aging "before your eyes."
Pines rippled with spasms: same old windy story.
You're wearing violet on your lids, dividing up the hours.
In the new stories, they give more lip and don't die.
His sentences don't move you, their obsidian reflections.
In all probability you'll never "gaze on him" again.
The sun flickers on and off, weary comic light bulb.
What's for dinner, what's for dinner, what's for dinner.
You're at the itchy trigger finger of a bony tale.
Riding Hood hungrily beds her wolf, then tames him.
Of course this is only one of thousands of refractions.

La Catrina

William Matthews (1943–1998)

The knotty question in my mind, awake at 5 AM,
is who will dominate the garden outside the window,
rooster or dog. I almost sense that the bougainvillea
shrinks from the fowl's cackling vibrations, the cur's
piteous incessant gulp of dusty air. And the sad cries
of grackles blackening the jardin? Melody indeed
compared with this barnacle of sound attached to sleep,
siesta, my shaky-under-the-best-of-conditions peace of mind.

The dream I'd been enjoying cut into by sharp scissors:
Airport, wobbling off a plane, and there's Bill
proffering white lilies, moment of such pleasure
(he was alive!) spliced into by the instrument
of rowdy brute sound. Such courteous people,
the Mexicans, raising such unruly animals.

Abounding in San Miguel, las flores—red, orange, yellow—
carried in white cotton by women, iris, lilies, daisies,
mums jumbled in the mercado, profusion for poquito
American dinero, sweet noisy color paid for
with gringa sleeplessness. Only in dream
would Bill bring flowers, though he bestowed
with an awkward grace sweet courtliness to his friends.

In the cobbled streets, I circumnavigate lovers
stitched silent, close. My god they're unmovable,
the young, not for them the calendar's death grin.
All the shops sell images of Calavera Catrina, skeleton
beauty queen in evening gown, décolletage all rib,
a bone danseuse arabesquing at fate. The Mexican
living eat mummy candy, the honeyed dead.

Outside my window, the unseen rooster, brouhaha.
I thought they only greeted dawn, but they can't stop
praising the day as it bracelets all our pursuits.
I hate the rooster's monotonous rumba squawks,
I want the dream back. This didn't start out elegiac,
a poem about a rooster, that's all. But as my guide
said yesterday, "Mexico's a strange place. The town—
Los Tilos, Lindens—doesn't have one linden tree
and never will." This is my small surprised rose
for you, Bill.

Persephone

Ghosts cannot cross your threshold unless you let them in.
— Margaret Atwood

When Mother died
her presence did not leave me for a while,
though it was not a ghostly thing. I spoke
to her but she did not answer. I held her
in my mind—memories so fresh I was sure
she would walk in and speak. I told time
by her watches, I wore her clothes. From
mirrors, she looked at me. Cheekbones,
shoulders, hands, feet, hair: hers. I see now
that I was the ghost. And I was a marked
woman, I understood that. I was on the road
she took. I did things "normally." My
husband did not know I had vanished yet.

In the distance
a car alarm bleats, then stops. Sundays
are quiet. I give thanks to religions
which sanctify the day, make all clamor stop.
Everything between a mother and a daughter
that needs to be uttered stays with me
in this room, I can hear the words. Most
of the sorrow is gone.

Burning

She has time to open drawers, turn
the contents upside down, fling them
into shopping bags, load the car
with paintings, bibelots, photos
of her family, travels and both
marriages. The faces of in-laws
whom she never sees or speaks to
smile from rooms she hasn't dreamed
about for years. Hills are burning;
the air makes her throat close,
ashes fall bone-gray on the car,
the sky is dark and yellow. A picture
spills from an envelope: young slim self
standing without clothes, golden skin
in golden light with the flat stomach
she remembers; it's not imagination.
Like a woman in a girlie magazine,
she wears too much makeup, gaze
sly and stony, pretending to be alone,
pretending to forget the camera
pointed at her body, the man
behind the lens. The girl she does
and doesn't want to look like is caught
forever. What to do with her?
Flames leap across canyons, trees
explode, animals flare up like torches.
The photograph stares at her and
she stares back, sure now she'll save it
from the fire, as she would any stranger.

Mood Sonnet #3

In the yellow part of day you heard Handel, or Purcell?
Today you can't enter the up-and-down marching of it.
The apple's on the table, stripped of connotations.
Green trooping in the trees, the blond of the path.
So you felt sad a while ago, you were writing a poem.
You actor of chimes, you pretender of madrigals.
Your wardrobe keeps some part of you an island.
Lunch is waiting in the basket, like a good fairy tale.
If you get lost, will you use the bread for a path?
Library of dreams, narrations of immortal desire.
The mind's valentine-tango with seductive effluvia.
Why stop gobbling for beauty, "however fleeting"?
Music seeps into your byways, your rivers, their dams.
Confusion blinds you: is the water topaz? blue-green?

Mood Sonnet #4

Is this the Dordogne? Caverns, but no goose liver in sight.
Was it a mistake to have postponed our carnal quadrille?
The peasants gather in the inn to mock our British accents.
My dear, explain that smudge of madness in your small locket.
Our quandaries, like children, drool themselves to sleep.
Ending up suburban, the mask we fear will blanket us.
We won't know 'til it's over which one of us will fade first.
Lust's Manifest Destiny working itself out though dolls.
To break out of a life you must have the humility to destroy it.
Some glass reflects only the eyesight's blind persistence.
Love-in-the-Mirror, so delightful, so beautifully coifed.
Waking up hung-over on the veranda of a vanishing horizon.
Dream-spell, manzanita-tangled, red and lonesome.
Sorry, the blahs cannot always be postponed, my Queen.

The Court Jester

Danny Kaye aka David Kaminski looked
Jewish so Sam Goldwyn, who thought

the goyim preferred looking at their own
on the big screen, made him dye his dark hair

and eyebrows reddish blonde. I love Danny's
pompadour. I admit I had a crush on him

when young. My father took me to see
The Court Jester, one of the few times

I can remember the two of us having fun. Oh
that Danny boy—his pirouettes and entréchats,

his racy-spacey tongue sputtering fractured French,
Italian, German. In jester tights his long slim legs

rested in third or fourth position, the few
seconds he wasn't in motion. Abracadabra!

Watch grace dissolve into campy gawkiness.
When the jester's knighted so he can be killed

in joust by burly Sir Griswold, the hours-long
ceremony has to be sped up to five minutes.

Danny's marched to and fro, right and left,
between rows of ironclad soldiers. His armor's

magnetized: he keeps banging into everyone.
He's held up, shuffling, between the strutting

guys, his knees and feet sticking out at right angles,
a plié in air. I laughed so hard I started coughing.

Daddy loved to point out each famous face
who was one of us: Kirk Douglas, Tony Curtis.

Danny, our blonde fool, tender, silly, our Jew.
Love scenes with Glenis Johns had no chemistry.

I didn't know from gay or bisexual then (hey,
I didn't even know about sex!) and if Daddy

had suspected he'd have made fun of him and
we wouldn't have gone. Dad reached for my hand

as we walked home from the theater.
I let him hold it.

How Am I Driving?

Was it because her father taught her how to ride a bike
that she'd now need training wheels if she'd ever ride
one, fat chance, and was it because her father taught
her how to drive that she flunked the driver's test
three times and it was only she thinks sometimes
because her lover talked her into buying a used black
Triumph convertible, car that he alone coveted but
couldn't afford, and because she got sick and tired of him
driving her and her car to the Rose Garden, to Tilden,
to Mendocino, town she always thought sounded
as if it and everyone one in it lied, remembering
Big Daddy's growling Mendacity, Mendacity
to Elizabeth Taylor and Paul Newman, that she finally
went out driving with a man she didn't know well,
kind despite the hiss of snakes tattooed on his biceps,
relearned to drive without a man yelling at her
or grabbing the wheel and took the test and passed
fine, just fine. It was not because of anyone
that she was, as a child, dyslexic, but it was probably
because her parents made her become a righty
when she was a lefty (she can tell because when
she throws a ball it's instinctively with the left)
that she still has trouble with directions. On
the other hand (which one? she's probably confused),
did her father's rants about Commies, workers
and blacks turn her into a lifelong pinko?
At the end, her dad died diapered and cribbed,
when she thinks of him today the equation of death
and time has subtracted most of her anger, not all,
certainly, but what's left is transformed into a kind
of victory: she lives peacefully in a world which he's left.
Now, as she drives up her canyon (over speed limits:

don't tell the cops)—his little left-wing, left-brain, his
little bird (not bird-brain), winging right, winging left,
left on her own, no limits but hers, getting older—
the future's talking back to her (no lie, no lie),
she's flying a narrowing corridor where what's left
is the certainty that he's the only father she'll ever have
and that she no longer needs one to love or to hate
or to assign cause to.

Legacy

Walking, or should I say wobbling, down Fifth,
   my aunt leans on a tri-wheeled contraption
that veers to the left while globs of teens scatter,
   and I hobble alongside with my sprained/strained/
weak ankle. We're quite a pair, I see,

by the stares of the kids, the turnings-away-of-the-head
   of polite matrons. My mother's knees were starting
to go, too, before she died. We're kind of flat
   footed, our gait passed down from the house
in the Ukraine, the piano, the French lessons,

the five proud daughters and the playboy father.
   And before these stories? (True? Half true?)
A whole family's past is whited-out. But
   that walk's been there for centuries, gimpy gals
in every generation. I'm trying to walk differently.

When young, you think you're so rare, so original,
   squinting out beyond the grown-up photographer
into the distance of your own sweet future.
   Parents are slim, keen (oh, how beautiful they
are!), no one yet knows of the knees or diabetes,

no one yet dreams of the cancer. Dim, back
   in Minsk or Warsaw, with the rest of the missing.
Good-bye to the shtetl or dacha, good-bye
   to thick black boots, gleaming proud piano.
Good-bye to dead babies, lost fathers, sisters

who die young. Good-bye poverty, good-bye
  Anti-Semites, farewell pogroms. Wave good-bye, too,
to the lump on the old auntie's breast, just forget
  all of it when you depart for the Brand New World.
My sister says we met my father's father once.

Legend has it he peddled fruit on Delancy Street.
  My father never talked about the past. My aunt
and I, a little unsteady island of connectedness,
  totter to the Met. Finally, what heritage
comes down to: knees, feet.

Mood Sonnet #5

for my sister

Unwavering bells ring out into the attenuated night.
The sleeper must decide not which dream came first, but primary.
Fire in the puppet theater: only two puppets not burned.
Immobile on their strings, their dresses brand-new.
The sleeper decides not to make a fuss in the forest of signs.
Hard to catalogue her drifts into polar regions, magnolias.
What most unsettles her: the on-again-off-again sun.
A butterfly rests in the teacup of her quiet hands.
Night pulses with milky light, warning her room.
Waking incessantly to the ruthless confident clamor of bells.
How does one explain if the world has gone tone-deaf?
Backstage has eighteen purpled corridors to get lost in.
Though it masks the dark places, her wig begins to fray.
After saving one puppet, she stumbles out of a door, lives.

Mood Sonnet #6

Archive of memory: chaotic, persistent, sly.
Boy chasing me around the lagoon, biting me hard.
Grandmother screaming. Tetanus shot, my shame.
The sail boats bobbed in their moorings, I pet a dog.
So the story's also another story of what came earlier.
Memory, recollection: can't say I remember Now.
Now has to wait a while until I think and arrange it.
I remember well the scrambled eggs at breakfast.
What about the orange juice, was that more important?
Place the frame around a gesture, shut the lens.
Enter in mid-sentence, exit at end of the next phase.
Is there an end to your revising, your regrets?
Play Catch the Quiddity, the game goes on and on.
The sky empty blue, I ran, he bit my arm: hurt.

Euphoria

Just when I've decided to work on
my attitude, i.e. get a better one,
a regatta of bouncing happy thoughts
on the rough but exhilarating sea of life,

when I've promised not to squander
the shrinking hoard of edenic moments
left to me, not to let time erode
the most far-out sexual memories

that make me and certain men
blush when we meet in the deli or street,
when I've vowed to immerse myself
(with *joie de vivre*) in serious study

of falconry or moths (not figuring
out how to keep them from eating
my clothes—but their miraculous
cycle of life!) or how goat cheese is made

(since I eat so much of it), and though,
let's face it, I've never evinced one iota
of interest in learning about these subjects,
the new me—the no more brooding, no regrets

me, the no more spaced out, daydreaming me,
will focus my feral attention outward
toward all the cheeses of the world. This
newly-minted me not only reads everything

on Tibet, Beijing, Darjeeling, she jets there
in her unwrinkleable unsinkable travel gear
whereupon she stuns her fellow explorers
with her recondite lore. This new me

accepts every solicitation to savor novel behavior,
however rococo. I'll go bowling, rowing,
contra dancing, learn dressage, chess, speak
Urdu, Mandarin, Portuguese (Mardi Gras!),

Farsi. I'll throw parties, entice guests
with nutrients I've actually cooked, yes,
I'll be a chef, put pomegranate seeds
on lettuce, fling cashews into soup, yes,

squeeze curlicues of peppers onto plates,
yes! yes! my parties will have nationalities—
Parisian soirees, Peruvian salons,
Come-As-Your-Favorite-River revels—

oh, I'm a new self-invention, breathless,
agog, I'll follow whatever paths
my ardors stumble upon, greet hazards
of luck's Lotto with gusto,

pluck, panache, zest!

             —And then I get the letter.

Clunk! That was a silver lining crashing
down from the thrashing clouds.

All bets are off,

the towel's thrown in, the slates wiped clean,
the horses won't run, the shops have shut down,
the toys put away, locked.

River Barge

Why did you pack that tie? I hate that thing.
  The porthole's open, breeze making a ruckus,
    sweeping air from port to starboard. If your
glance grows cooler, I'll surely need a blanket.
  Will this xylophone morning thwonk us
    a new theme? Time to admire Landscape
scrolling by—diamonded river, sweep of grass,
  Monet rolls of hay. Don't you think the yellow

bedspread's tacky? Shared disdain takes us
  for a ride on the rowdy train of sex. The always
    erotic future. Yeah, yeah. Lust, that laser,
still bores in on us, but I'm not misled
  by generalities. Once such rakish mysteries
    to each other, we almost broke up in Paris!
Cute little sparrows skittered among ivied sculptures,
  schoolgirls cartwheeled, and we recited injuries.

What scholars we were of each other's failures,
  our disquisitions perfectly Talmudic.
    The air hummed with a circus-like energy.
On our barge they feed us caviar and rabbit. God,
  the river's Valium calm gets on my nerves!
    Even voicing an opinion's dangerous. I never
knew you felt that strongly about Muscadet, or
  Delacroix, and I certainly did not mean it literally
    when I threatened to jump overboard and
swim home alone.

Aging Trip

Irreversible clot that creeps through the body, weakens it
inside and out, and she hates it, hates giving in
to the momentum, the traveling invisible mote
of missing wineglasses, sleeves with strings hanging,
messy and unnerving. She lies in bed mornings
counting the injured and slow-healing parts, meanwhile
her cholesterol's rising, rising like a mad yeast, what
an orchard of clumsy reproachable prunings she is,
not to speak of what's happening to her face, waist,
and she knows she's forgotten for the moment (memory's
player piano with the old familiar tunes starting to disappear)
all the other stuff, aches in hands, back—and her eyesight—
don't ask! When she was a child, her grandmother, plump
cozy woman, waltzed alone, whirling in the living room,
belting songs as the child looked on incredulously
and with embarrassment. Younger than springtime am I.
Grandma!

So, what's with it between the spirit and the body?
Which one leads? Which one's got it right? Spirit and Body
separating, waving sadly, lovingly at each other, as the ship,
with the gravity of a grandfather, leaves the pier with only Body
on board. Diva of dust, wrapped up on deck in fur, pashmina,
the finest wool, she's trying to keep warm in the sea-cold,
remain in the sun's favor. The sun, of course, has its own
compulsion as it moves down through the sky's river,
and, as they leave the harbor, is beginning to slowly dip
into the horizon. It's only Spirit, on shore, who suspects
the ship's final port of call. Body holds her stomach in
staunchly, throws her fur shawl around her shoulders,
marches into dinner, looks around for the good-looking men.

Selected Dreams from the Animal Kingdom

The dog dream was interrupted because of hunters
pretending to be owls, at 6 AM. How dumb
do they think bucks are? Later, six deer
ambled onto the lawn from fields, nibbled
on box elders. Two cats ogled them,
cows' heads swiveled, did their big-eyed
stare, stilled like enormous milk pitchers
but all animals stayed cool in this version
of the Peaceable Kingdom, I, standing at the door,
included. Maybe that's why I had dog dreams.
My quilted version of things starred a huge
husky Ulysses—wandering dog, hunter.
Just like my lover, he of the wandering eye.

Box elders make an excellent picnic for deer,
but those box elder bugs get on one's nerves,
reddish, crawling toward the light and heat,
creeping up blinds and mirrors, even—yikes—
coffee cups. Going everywhere they shouldn't.
Completely ugh. I've done a purge on them,
broomed them to death. Ulysses, propped
up on hind legs, paws placed on my shoulders,
said, with an intense mien, "I like your hair."
Though I allowed him to nose and nuzzle
my locks, when Ulysses was unleashed, he ran away.

This dream's too obvious to analyze. In so-called
Real Life (the one not supposed to be a dream),
I knew my shrink did not like this guy. Q: How
do we know these things? A: Sometimes
they don't control their tone of voice when
speaking of an actor in one of your Soaps.

After I'd decided to turn the man loose, to
roam the whole fucking world if he wished to,
frolic with Circe or a Siren (though wasn't
that me?) I basked in my shrink's respect—
a small consolation for the loss of love.

It's fall, hunters run loose. I rove the hills
in cap and vest, bright orange, a color
I detest, but don't want to be dead meat
as I suspect the buck is. (That deer family
nibbling on the trees consisted of two does,
four fawns—no buck to be seen.) Or if not
dead, hunted down, he could be wandering,
making whoopee with a new doe, possibly
to turn up in that doe's dream someday,
maybe as a man, a hunter?

Mood Sonnet #7

The waiter leered, "The turbot is better tonight, Madame."
Scary to wear pale yellow silk around such curly aggression.
Like a pasha, the fat suede banquette dominated the room.
Even that lettuce in her *tricolore* salad had razory edges.
On her tippy-top shelf stand all the older lurks of poetry.
How can she reach for Pope, for Rilke, if her back hurts?
The new neighbors' lawn perfect as the first assignation.
Now her heart's Little Engine That Could: sputter-sputter.
She rakes lovingly through a pile of messy fallen words.
From inside the clothes closet, festoonings of civil war.
Take the blue coat, whining with boredom, for its walk.
Each of Madame's garments so ambitious for redolent deeds.
They've made it too easy to have fun in this century.
"That salad could use more vinaigrette. Or etiquette."

Mood Sonnet #8

Ocean-liner burdened with past caught and hunted down.
Life we can expect: unguarded irises crumbling into stars.
What's on for evening's casual yet elegant isolation?
Try And Navigate the undertow of the heart's longings.
The sky's a lovely tiger, soignée with striped detail.
Words words spread randomly across, eroticism.
All that moves moist-heavy, seeking a tornado of kiss.
Exact music recalled *con spirito* I don't want to speak.
My hair blown into my mouth tangles my participation.
Night dreams not so obedient, young dogs chasing itches.
Each gangway opens up into blank face, hard, insensible.
Morning berry clouds bleat a chorus of little lamb song.
Hoist the flag and button up for the bugler's tatatata!
I've always loved sea voyages, the story retold, retold, retold.

The Mystery of Teeth

Is that a butterfly or moth? Should I praise
or mouth disgust? To the left, to the right.

Choose one. Difficult to pick which lipstick—
sassy red-brown (Monsoon Madness), prissy

coral-pink (Breath of Innocence)—so use both,
be sassy-prissy. It used to be called lip rouge.

Now you twist silver cylinders and don't get
colored fingers. I'm such a fashion floozy,

walking down the main street of a Western town
("Main Street"), enticed by the splashy window

(saddles, bridles, blue suede cowboy boots)
of a riding goods store. So I don't ride, sue me.

Down the long, dimly-lit aisle silver spurs
preen & flash, & I wonder: could I attach a pair

of spurs to my Nikes? Flit over to a row
of ranchers' rubber coats, tip-of-boot length.

Just the thing for driving sportively
to the Farmer's Market in an LA drizzle!

Hey, you're either a Hungerer, or you are not.
To the left, to the right. Choose one. We'll

give you the correct answer later. A friend
rides into Sheridan with her cute puppy Iris,

wearing a silver pin that looks like Iris. At
home, she puts a wineglass down on a cork

coaster, a cut-out figure of an Iris-type dog.
A big puppy head. When my friend's

in the shower, Iris chews on her dog bed,
but sometimes, feeling mischievous, she

sneaks into the living room & chows down
on her corky likeness. In ignorance, of course,

of the deep connection between herself
& a coaster.

Signal for the Eerie Light

Cindra explains why coffee in a small cup cools
   faster than in a large cup, according to Newton's
theory. My brain falls into deep blank repose.
   While other people drive bravely down the backroads
of black holes or the periodic table with their brights on,
   I creep blindly with mine dimmed. Really, I try,
diligently scanning articles on WIMPS and MACHOS,

the iridescence of copper, DNA's vines tangling
   through our elaborate bodies. Presto! Before heat's
escaped from my magical cup, the ideas behind
   the splendid names have been rabbited away. Is
it in my genes? Is that why I studied principles
   of astrology—Planets, Houses, Rising Signs, Oppositions!—
casting charts, impressing even myself with my insight?

Betty, a Marxist-Leninist-slash-Astrology Practitioner
   like me, thought the Stars preened with knifelike accuracy:
I saw the system as a neat setup for seductions.
   When men entered my small room for a reading,
I could foresee brilliantly the future of his next hour
   or so! How real and unreal ideas are. I was seventeen
when Arnie, twenty-three, revealed that as a serious person

I had to choose between faith in God and atheism, I
   couldn't be agnostic. Wanting him to love me forever,
I chose the void. A year before, I'd perused books
   on the fancy Catholic Faith. It was the cadences
I wanted to conjure that hover in the pause,
   the silence, waiting. Only now I'm remembering
that for hours I practiced sorcery in my frou-frou

girl's room, waved gold and blue scarves, tried to
    move pencils with my mind, waited for the brindling
of light itself to show me the true art of what's
    unknowable. I never learned the secrets of prestidigitation.
They called me to dinner whereupon I opened the door
    and walked dazedly down the long bright hall
lit by the enchantment — of electricity.

Mood Sonnet #9

Those potted-palm days of Edwardian glamour.
A wave of your pale glove, my lace-bordered sleeve.
Let's be spirits again, take the air on the Promenade.
Find that slow hotel room, with the window unlatched.
Lovely the falling and rising of compatible bodies.
At the top of the Wheel, world fades into truth.
Breeze grazes my cheek from conscience's sad island.
Below, small as a violet your wife's corseted form.
Is not erotic drama a crusade, holy and violent?
A place real as theater, to which I'll not return soon.
The egg of longing balancing on my open palm.
Our feathery costumes sun on the curious stones.
I want you to know when my heart hurt the most.
It hurt most when I made myself fade into sepia.

Mood Sonnet #10

Let's take our cues from shiny black Japanese dishes.
"There's nothing that gives more assurance than a mask."
Clothed in Venetian panoply, we're radiant refugees.
Haven't we wanted to escape every North Pole?
As long as we don't get zonked out on sentimental detritus.
All that babble about "naked souls;" mere hooks and snares.
Olympia on her hard bed more dressed up than anyone.
Brazen confident stare—and her nipples wink as well.
City a blue wilderness where the cougar hunts us down.
Swallow the bittersweet pill, jump in bed with the doctor.
Luxe Amazonian shivers, Mississippian ribbons and bells.
"The calla lilies are in blossom again. Such a strange flower."
Snap goes photo-memory, click-click and the date.
City sings us its silky oratorio while sky ticks misalliance.

II

Life? Literature? One to be made into the other?

—Virginia Woolf

The Secret Life of a Cloud

Release me, O ye gods, from the de-turquoised
facts of life. Why isn't food more interactive today?
Why are the boiled eggs waxy, lethargic? I want
the nectarines to start juggling themselves. I want
to see fruit cartwheeling around my prosy kitchen.
The world scarcely exists for us mind-sinners, lovers
of our own thoughts far more than we love God.

Let V stand in for fact. See V out the window. Or
is it WV? Weathervane, wither vain; why vow?
I think I'll just go on twirling reality like a rhinestone
baton. Birches march in rows like the proud defeated,
or exiles. Tomorrow they may be necklace giraffes.

Sugar pantry of dreams, a child glutton's, and early on,
a marshmallow is Paradise Toasted. But I've fallen.
Now, it's scary food, glutinous and pallid. Learn
to recognize seepages. Look them straight in the eyetooth.
This music crept by us upon the watermelon.

Shiny CIA piano spreads out into my sanctum,
fat-assed with tiny white ballerina shoes. Player piano
with attitude, expounding on each and every calorie
of my brie en croute panini. Yes, I often eat
standing up—so do trees.

A Tale of a Tutu

It was too wrenching to think about the tutu
locked away in a closet, pink cotton candy tulle
smudged from practicing multiple lifts.

(Or smirched by wandering hands?) *Francesca,*
Madame Lionesse warned repeatedly (she
of the grand Russian school of fouettés and

port de bras), *stay away from those filthy boys!*
Gypsies, pfou, pfou! Her black penciled eye-
brows popping up to touch the yellowed hair

pulled into a flat bun. (Francesca knew Madame
peroxided. Wasn't she ancient—thirty, forty?)
Francesca sneered while doing battements.

How enchanting the tutu, that blushing uniform,
how it felt breathlessly tight around bust
and waist, erupting bouffant at narrow hips.

Wearing it, she was a lily, a bon-bon, a glass
of pink champagne. Madame banned it for a month.
For you, Francesca, it is the black leotard!

Absolutement! Now Francesca danced black,
thought black. It wasn't fair! That sly cow
Daphne met her lover Boris every night

bourréeing down the hall to the danseurs' rooms.
Daphne and Boris pas de deuxed divinely. Madame
noticed only *that* effect of Daphne's nocturnal wanderings.

Ha, thought Francesca, wait 'til Daphne's gone
a few more months, and Boris can't raise her past his chest.
A puny Albrecht and a fat, pregnant Giselle!

The pink tutu, so adorable, Paco'd say, when
you wear it you are a Christmas ornament, I want
to sprinkle you with tinsel. Then as his hands

reached inside her bodice, the two would
dance their vernal secret. *You're a goddess.*
But that damned Madame, watching, watching,

the lights of the studio reflected in her pendant nose.
(Madame eschews powder, it makes her achoo.)
And Paco hoists his body onto Francesca's no more.

Oh it's boring to feel sorry for yourself too long.
She's jumping higher, faster. And no one's
lifting her. A new garment's caught her eye —

serpent green moiré — more her type, now
that she's lived through *the death of love.*
She thinks a turban, too, might suit her.

Alluring mysterious shadows circle her eyes.
Caught in imagination's witchery, she thinks
the moon's a cabbage rose, a little tattery, a little tricky.

Mood Sonnet #11

August farrago of novels, sweat, persimmons, slumber.
Fan's circling, buzzing in the soporific hazy morning.
Wearing soggy shorts and T-shirt, guzzling lemonade.
Oh joy of honeysuckle, Ping-Pong, Trollope, summer lips.
Ten years ago, she moved into a house she still resorts to.
Correction: *they* moved in before she implored him to leave.
Divorce entails much shoving around of heavy furnishings.
Out with old straight-backed chair, in with new mink chaise.
Novelty of the lover: jump in wearing your flimsiest corset.
Having been sent her poetic efforts, he leaves them in Dorset.
Another reason she gets rid of him: he reminds her of Dad.
Fashion Tan streaks the instep of her (dainty) left foot.
All three men must go before she can be a poet, hey-ho!
"Whatever fantods you scribble, vaunt them in a barouche."

Mood Sonnet #12

The day squeezes anxious yellow from white and gray.
Sun, if you've a bone to pick—put up your Miami dukes.
Fuzzy scraps and tatters of nocturnal tumblings.
Yeah, there's the dream world, its epigrammatic truth.
From the mythic to the comic: were they always the same?
Never said I was a housewife, never promised to bake one thing.
Corners of memories, dusty, in need of a good sweeping.
When even the weather seems to collude with history.
Is distraction a good search-engine for discovery?
Mind plays Scrabble, scrambling: tessara or terrazzo.
I'm no archaeologist, only a writer waiting for language.
Hard to determine which part's nylon, which magic.
A soul ain't free after the form's been invented.
Comb reality's mane until it's silky: Sit. Lie down. Fetch.

Love in the Tenth Century

Watching the moon
at dawn,
solitary, mid-sky,
I knew myself completely,
no part left out.
            —Izumi Shikabu

Their love-making, they agree, mingles sorrow
with joy. They speak this while overlooking the tiny
artificial lake and well-proportioned, man-made hill.

Before the moon vanishes, he slips back to his house,
where wives and concubines sleep, he hopes alone,
where he must immediately write that tanka

praising the night of bliss, his wondrous mistress.
Perhaps he'll mention hair that reaches to her knees,
or face carved like the silver moon, or

compare her body to the curves of the hill.
He has five lines, thirty-one syllables:
what good manners and custom require.

She waits eagerly to receive proof
of the elegance of his mind, and to examine
his writing (is it well-shaped, refined?)

before writing back a tanka while the sun rises.
Now in their own houses, satiated, safe,
their meeting a luxurious secret (shared

by a dozen attendants or so). Before they meet
again, verses blaze between them. The messengers,
intrigued, sneak peeks and secretly believe

their poet's best. His: more classically
pure, hers: more deft. The next liaison, inflamed
by all those words—a conflagration!

Nights for a year: brief discussions on the fleeting
world, the fading moon, etc., etc.
The tankas praise each other's secret places.

But the husband's brother-in-law, prime minister,
mentions (casually) one day at court: "My sister
hasn't looked well or happy this year, I wonder why?"

She writes now for no one but herself. Tankas
spill from her pen. What great poets write
about—autumn, or snow, or late blossoms—

should not only be beautiful, bring pleasure,
but should hurt. How did this elude her?
The moon widens as she watches it.

Tears

When parting with a man with whom
you have sworn love, it is most inconvenient
if you cannot shed tears.

—*Tickling Grass*, instruction book for courtesans, 1654

Instructed to think of sad things
from her own life—to make her weep
so he'll go away pleased—she
fakes the feeling, makes
a scene. The experts' advice
for young courtesans not acquainted
with life's sorrows: pull out
your eyelashes.

The Edo man-about-town brags
to other men: Have you seen
my collection of love testaments?
Sealed with, even written in,
courtesan blood. Women
learn to prick their gums
painlessly with sharpened quince,
a kind of eighteenth-century toothpick.

Insecurity escalates. Love's test:
a lock of her lacquered hair. Next,
a tattoo of his name on her shoulder.
Then he wants the woman's
fingernail. A *shinju*—sincere proof
of love. Finally, the way
a courtesan shows she cares:
she gives the biggest spender
her severed finger.

But a hand has only five fingers,
and there are too many men!
High-ranked courtesans of the Yoshiwara,
so resourceful, purchase love-nails
and love-fingers from graveyards.

What if she's just an ordinary whore?
She can be forced—for special monetary
favors—to chop off special fingers.
One woman's small digit
flies out the window from the blow,
gets lost in the garden's waters. Her
lover says, you've given it to another
man. She must offer another one.

Their love not sanctioned, he's in disgrace.
The Afterlife looks better every day.
With his knife at her throat, what can she do
but open her neck to him?

How sad he fell in love with his courtesan,
people say, how affecting. Behind
her screen, a married woman, sleepless,
alone, reads the stories of wild intractable love,
and weeps.

Mood Sonnet #13

Pink, last year's color, doesn't suit me.
O razzy expressions, pearl-buttons of praise.
Seduction's fascination, why it doesn't need fact.
We weren't going anywhere until you stood still.
Our baggy secret made out of shiny material.
The leaves hanging on as if winter's a lie.
As I said, pink doesn't show off my complexion.
Did you think you had all the time in the world?
Desire refracts into lace, porous as a mantilla.
Saying goodbye? Easier said than staying gone.
Speaking Swedish not always a snap for my tongue.
So bring on the ritual: shop for better-titled clothes.
Aka the refreshment of a soul's reconstruction.
The early bird sings, "Wear blue, my dear, wear blue."

Mood Sonnet #14

Near the sandy plains of sleep, the sea curls, uncurls.
Hear the heart open in a corridor of doors.
If dreams don't plot I'll play this one out to its sweet end.
Me Jane with pre-fire Rochester, the hunky liar.
Don't think I can wait for this book to compose itself.
My mind hat's pouting on my head, a pert come-on.
Lacking aplomb, my ploy is to mad-taxi into drama.
Sky's black market pusher, its blank glitter, lust.
The willow-choir twitches and quivers like maidens.
Call in your dream surgeon and save someone's life.
"Hero Talks Jane Into Giving Him Long Mortgage."
Others of us promise to become Pilgrims, to roam.
His pleated cheek and arm from the fire's paintbrush.
Just pray night's denouement won't cut each love away.

Famous Pairs

Adam and Eve strolled through Paradise, innocent, in the dark.
One bite: the Fall, then misery, and Satan creeps in the dark.

Mark Antony's gone. Cleopatra puts the asp to her breast.
Iris, Charmian expire. Cleo dies too. The snake's replete in the dark.

All Salem's come out to gawk at Hester's fashion statement.
Her sin's exposed, while Dimmesdale clasps his secret in the dark.

Mimi needs a little oil for her lamp and Rudolph's happy to supply.
But love can't cure that cough. Forever she sleeps in the dark.

Charles Baudelaire loves Jeanne Duval. Hates her too:
she's panther, incubus, vampire who shrieks in the dark.

Marcel waits impatiently in bed for his Mother's kiss.
A footstep! Here she is! Still, his heart's incomplete in the dark.

When Anais met Henry, it was like looking in a mirror—
Lust or vanity? Is it self-love or sympathy that speaks in the dark?

Rhett wants Scarlett, Scarlett wants Tara, Sherman burns Tara,
Scarlett thinks about it tomorra. Rhettless, she weeps in the dark.

Holofernes the Philistine beds Judith and gets a big surprise.
She'd said, "Shall I lie down with you, my sweet? In the dark?"

Big Mouth

If I speak in a whisper, dear Orpheus, it's because
I've had too many cigarettes plus I don't want to spook you
since I am sort of a spook.

What a monsoon of tears you've shed mourning me.
For my part, I have to tell you Hell's gloomy and moonless,
it's hard to read newsprint
and I missed my cell phone,
and though at times when I was alive
I thought I'd kill you when you snored at night,
the recollected cacophony of your sounds obsessed me.

Honey, it did. Keep up the pace. Don't mind me
chattering behind you.

You have to do something to keep
your sprits up in Hades. Some of the male shades down there
were shameless flirts. A few times, I must admit,
I was tempted,
I mean it's so dark and all, what's a girl to do but sleep
and screw, but unlike a certain person I won't mention
(her name rhymes with Ellen), I remained
loyal to you by doing the Salute to the Sun
Stretch when my libido yenned.

I could have posed for a frieze of fidelity.
While the others staggered around, bandaged with wine
and coke, I arranged my shoes by color.

When Poseidon came for dinner, what an El Niño
of longing! The girls practiced their swan dives, hoped their thongs
would come off when they hit the water.
I hung around the pool in my modest cutoffs.
The guys flung me in, though,
and I guess they could see my tits through
my wet T-shirt.

Because Poseidon asked me out. All the girls, especially
that awful Ellen of Troy, were disappointed
but I was the princess with the slipper that fit.
Plus you were taking a hell of a long time to fetch me.

OK, OK, I'll tell you about this Poseidon. Very cute,
long gray beard, very good abs, left his pitchfork
or whatever that pronged thing was at home
when we went out for sushi.
Raw fish such a pleasure after all that barbecue.
We talked about deep things. Like I can't remember now.

Hey, Orph, keep on walking up the stairs.

You know how you and I had some sexual issues.
You weren't there to address them, so Poseidon helped me
work them out. New techniques like
Riding the Waves. The Plunge. Strawberry Jam. And hon,
did you know men could give head, too?

I thought you'd be pleased!

This is a very delicate time in our relationship.
I want to go home
right now!

Accoutréments

—after the female Surrealist painters

I am the little desk on which you carve your name. I am the leather boots in which you wriggle your toes. I am the blue chair you sit on when you sip your tea and think. The mirror you gaze into is my adoration. You wipe your mouth on me when you use a napkin. I am your bath water. Don't forget to clip your beard with me. The silk shirt you wear out to dinners? My skin.

My wit is the knife you cut your bread with. The lamp you read by is my insight. When you fall into your soft bed (me) your dream becomes my poem.

Mood Sonnet # 15

Here on Kings Mountain the unstable sun's dismaying.
The path twines itself crazy like Ariadne's string.
We hikers know well the story of the burned-out barn wraith.
Bring a sandwich, the twilight mountain lion might be hungry.
And a suitcase, in case you meet a rock star and he wants a date.
In these parts, the most famous denizen's a talking gorilla.
You go around a bend and, Hello, here's Koko: I WANT BANANA.
Koko, we saw two banana slugs mate motionless on a shiny leaf.
Sometimes that's the way you want to do it, static-graceful.
Try Five Card Stud if you get lost, but Canasta don't win no tiara.
I'm definitely the least-known creature on this mountain.
Might this be a lotus dream floating up from my lonely youth?
My empty-room bravado stripped down to its foundation.
While others are ruined by publicity, I'm bone-ivory, saved.

Mood Sonnet #16

I come from a place where the rituals are exported.
I ask the jury, should I love my childhood more?
Cruelty's such instructive food, while kindness slims.
I look for doorways that shine in the dark, mirrors.
Wait for nights like horses, unbridled, at liberty.
Choosing this one and that one to kiss again.
As Queen, I command winter: Flower softly down.
My fondest reveries? Curvy, operatic. Gold-glinted.
Imagination's music requires such crocheted attention.
State dinners where ghosts truly learn to enjoy food.
Is this questionnaire as real as my thoughts?
I'll stay truthful except when donning leopard spots.
If day becomes bloodshot, bathe, breathe, collect islands.
Darkness the best lighting for a connoisseur of rue.

The Bride Cake

Don't come in, the bride cake isn't ready,
Lord knows the sprinkles haven't dried,
not to speak of the snow-white spangles
that adorn the bride dress, they do not adorn
it yet. Don't come in with those sly hips. Stop
that! I have to sew and bake at the same time.

The whole household's in a tizzy, your
cousin's beside herself, weeping joy-tears,
dawdling at her dressing table, dreaming
of gondolas, piazzas, Tinteretto, and
her bridegroom's willy. Sixty jeroboams
of the fizziest champagne arrived by post coach

from London. If the guests do not consume all,
we servants will have our own festivities:
fare-thee-well to our spoiled miss, her
fits and fancies, her faints and feints.
The maids won't miss fixing that frizzy hair
in the manner of Lady Fitzroy or Teazle.

Sixty thousand pounds turn any young
heiress—plain as a pin, fleshless, certainly
melancholic—into a prize. Keep your hands off me,
young sir, this cake has ten tiers, I have to stack
each on top of each, like hat boxes, they mustn't
totter, this cake has to last at least one whole day.

We'll cut it carefully: jewel each guest will take
a slice of, concoction of dreams. On my attic cot,
I, too, envision an honest cavalier. As I roast
a bird, he'll snatch me up, convey me
to church, Baden-Baden, Rome, then home
resplendent, mistress of my own body and domain.

No, sir, I have no hopes of that from your direction.
But I'm thinking I might want some little gift
for what you've been getting free. Not just a box
of chocolates. Nor colored stockings. I'd like
some cold hard cash, sir, that's the ticket
if you ever wish again to tickle my tasket.

Look, Miss Havisham's drifting down
the staircase in lace, topaz eyes aburn, aglitter,
and like all brides, she's both triumphant and
plucked. The guests have arrived. The cake's
tiered, topped, and ready. But the ceremony
can't begin until a bridegroom appears.

Age of Ice

In old Peru swallows loitered in the ruined abbey
waiting for the prioress, Sister Evitita, to return.
Having not heard the bells do their ivory toil
for a while, they missed rising *ensemble*
and all the pretty aerial maneuvers they'd execute
showing off as the nuns gathered, their flying
buttress headdresses slanting upward as they watched
the birds loop-the-loop and play tag-tail. These
birds were aware of audience: they'd been planning
an exploratory foray to Hollywood when the nuns,
wimples and all, disappeared.

Thus began The Age of Ice, with all the attendant
triumphs and tragedies that accompanied
that resplendent epoch. This was the period
of the Samba of the Infanta, when minerals posed
as miniature tulips, and the people were happy
to be fooled in this manner as well as others.

Meanwhile, the swallows waited in a shallow lagoon,
having abandoned the abbey to get away from the heat.
For this was also the Age of the Furnace, paradox inherent
in the ways of God. In some spaces of the evening,
ghosts of ancient nuns were said to walk, svelte now,
from posing for portraits of the saints, becoming all
self-conscious and gawky. At dawn, they abandoned
the ruined abbey for cascading daydreams of becoming
supermodels. They picked names like Patient Griselda
and Tawny, dressed for success. They precursed the nuns
who by the way had gone to Hollywood in Sister
Evitita's train, this idea being in the air so to speak.

Try stopping the ways of culture, only culture knows
for certain what hope-fragments will be lopped off
from the bulk of human yearning, to be preserved
and raised up and war shipped. Having an attack of nerves?
What makes the world tolerable is a glossy magazine.
The room empty tonight, except for tin tiaras and
our quaint awareness of personal crusades. It
doesn't matter whom you take your lessons from,
swallows, nuns, dog shows, our business is to master
our little aromas with as much dignity as we can.

Mood Sonnet #17

Fall dulls into December, where do shadows hide?
Everything flat, on the same plane, frieze of the dead.
Once, people wore desire's barbs without irony.
The Greeks understood the need for flighty gods, for change.
Hunger unpacks her wardrobe, the mildewed clothes.
Only your most expensive shoes can comprehend want.
Little fraidycat, so scared of the mirror you've lost it.
Your likeness escorted to parties with too much cake.
Asking urgent questions of all the masks, in Finnish.
Mouth wants to say, O wine of Eros, O terror of love.
It also wants to ask if you can have seconds or thirds.
So what will do it for you: a never-ending erotic film?
Watch each image of love lost to others' wolfings.
Dream merged with remembrance licks the spoon clean.

Mood Sonnet #18

Either too hot, too cold, too spicy, too bland, too too.
Button-sweater terror as sun blazes your arm.
Resist what's inevitable, as if you were Queen.
All illusions flickering off the trees one by one.
Leaves fall: trite imagery or you're Japanese.
Escape, not to an era, but to the panther museum.
Love's petals fold themselves around the feral center.
Given one piece of the aromatic to gnaw on for a time.
Snowflakes go on babbling: the mad idea of spring.
Couples waltz to music hummed in polka-dots, chinz.
Why, in night's middle do you stop all the clocks?
Embarrass friends while you weep about your neck?
Reading life as if traveling in a car driven by another.
Breakfast's laughter: pure, itself. Day moves in, written.

Evil Muses

The ice-storm cometh, that was the prediction. Today the roofs shine in the sun's pretty enamel. Are we expected to make sense of this? Ring out the bell-bottoms, get someone else to do it. It's archery day at the writer's retreat. Impress us! Take aim at reality: twang through your suspension of disbelief.

Now we know you love your pets the reptiles but, dearie, how naïve can you get? When you lost their food (the rat hid behind the stove), one bit you—hard. Thus ended your snake-dancing. We'll wear feathers, but not boas.

At the border of your imagination is a region into which we parachute, spray-painting the earth with your blood. We assign all language here. We slam you down if you can't extricate yourself with a tango-Argentina si si syncopation.

Early on, we saw your integrity melt, puddling us as it sloped off the roof. We kept silent about it, gloating.

Practicing

We never thought to disobey the Duke our father,
though the strictures he lay upon our behavior
we hardly thought a blessing, but as the wind

looped around our ears & the cottonwoods tinkled
glass-like, we knew without words, for we were twins,
that this day had been chosen by us as rehearsal

for much more. Taking castanets down from the wall,
from the closet shoes with silver bows, we clicked
the instruments, stamped our feet in unison

just as Madame La Valencia had taught us,
though she was banished from the Duchy
for teaching us the Dance as well as Latin.

How this flamenco enflamed us, & we pinned
our hopes on more flamboyance, but we had
to wait until the next time Father left the castle.

Danger is an art, Annabelle said as we untied
the shimmering shoes & wiped our bodies
clean of sweat. *It is in our blood*, I said.

One month later, Father, called away to a remote part
of Romand, left us in the care of Beatrice, eighty,
half-blind, cataracts like clouds in both her old eyes

& we weren't spring chickens either,
being thirty-three that year, born one minute apart
by a weakened Mother whom we never knew.

Now Beatrice spent her time singing lullabies
to the memory of the babes born a reflection of the other,
black caul draped over both small foreheads,

despite which Annabelle & I sensed that we were beauties,
for Father said we were as rare in nature as black roses,
& we had seen the looks of knights, of valets, & of stable boys.

We would not say it aloud, but our shared vision
might have been summed up as Now Or Never.
for Father wanted us to stay virgins-manqué,

be his bridge partners (the cleric making up
the fourth), & most of all to waft around the castle
conjuring up his dead wife. Lightning rods for his memories,

we were weary of the practices which led to removal
of our clothing in those late candled evenings
when his nostalgia grew rich & glittering & potent.

It was to the stables that we proceeded on the eve
that Father left us to find reclining in their quarters
Louis, Nicholas, & Frederick, & oh how shocked

they were to see us enter trailing Spanish shawls
splashed with roses black & hot which burned us,
wearing white shifts & silver dancing shoes,

a look we knew successful having practiced on our Father
when in his cups he forgot he had banished dancing.
Louis pulled out his tambourine, & the stables

echoed with our fluid stamping. Then Annabelle & I
took Louis, Nicholas, & Frederick into an empty stall
& had the time-honored *droit des princesses* way with them.

When Father returned home from the hinterlands,
he called for us to come to him, as he was "tired,"
but we were miles away, riding swiftly on five fine horses

stolen from the Duchy stables by our three shared lovers
with whom we move from town to town performing dances
for gold & silver. Nights are our own that we light up

with *ballets erotiques* & we do not think it unkind
if we never write a thank-you note to Father
for his thoughtfulness in teaching us our natural practices.

Mood Sonnet #19

Swollen sleep-softened river of nerves we float down.
When you sense you are Starting to Travel to Fiji.
Hollow eroticism, that wider and deeper drowning.
Grasp for the dream-truth before light cracks your search.
You don't know French? Be Isabel Adjani, or snore.
Place hands over eyes when his nails quiver.
Innocence, self-sacrifice, weariness? Evil grabs her.
The hero sleeps, the hero's sick; mama's good boy.
Promises aren't promises, merely good manners.
When the daylight lover shows, consign him to night.
As he gorges, blood-pearls necklace the silvering skin.
In monsters you study what's underneath your fears.
Perform triangulated dream surgeries, or is it sugaries.
Kind people warn you before you get bitten, gone.

Mood Sonnet #20

No, this spread of cards does not look good at all.
Breathe through your nose, stifle the fear-hour.
I invite Colette for tea to teach me about L'Amour.
She regales me in thick Burgundy-inflected French.
I can only surmise—life's more fun if you're famous.
Oh, my little locket: fading cameo, blurring profile.
Sob, says vanity, bye-bye, waves to me from the waves.
For lifetimes I've missed you, Lady Izumi Shikabu.
Were we intimates, or was I your illiterate servant?
I feel a narrow bridge to you today, but it's a bit fatigued.
The sun of the heart returns then leaves too soon.
When light shifts its weight, mood somersaults.
And pulsing through the membranes of my eyelids.
The music of the moon's pallid victrola, longing.

Get to Know Your Soil

Something's in my jacket, fallen though
a pocket, a plastic spoon. I won't need it
on this walk past aluminum trailers, dogs
straining on chains, reindeer with ribbons
tied around fake fur necks. The air's dry,
crows fly over the field, one cries and
I hope the other answers the question posed.
Just follow me while I disappear
into the tenth century. I'm at the Heian court
in old Kyoto. Women judge would-be
lovers on the basis of their skills: archery,
painting, poetry, handwriting, how artfully
they layer their robes, lemon over rose
over sea-green over white, everyone
at court a little poetry machine, writing
out their lives. The Heian culture is so cute.
I hope the modern Japanese won't mind me
saying that, but after all, they invented Hello
Kitty, Pokemon and mechanical plastic pets
that "expire" if kids don't "feed" them.
If I use "cute" people look at me as if I'm
an idiot, when what I really mean is wonderful,
a word now utterly devoid of wonder.
Such a pity I can't always live in a book.
I like life's facts bleached like bones
in the high desert of the imagination,
also like lying, something I never did well
when young, selling off to the betrayers,
mom and dad, all my secrets. I might
be lying now. Heian people wrote poems
to love's pleasures, to its heartlessness,
praise of the emperor poems, leaving

the court poems (sad), they wrote
just-before-you-die poems (stoic), used
words—wind, moon, cricket, mountain,
snow, willow, dew—again and again,
shimmered them with desire, loss,
resignation. I wanted to put simple names
for the world into my poem, arrow them
high, like they did in the tenth century,
but this poem's coming on a country road
at the beginning of the twenty-first
at a place where I need to put on sunglasses
as the sun goes down to make the pinks glow
even more gorgeous next to the grays,
to tune my motor till it hums oddly,
and when clear nights visit
over the blue-tinged mountains, I say,
Hey, wonderful, what a cute moon.

Notes

The tanka which is the second epigraph to Part I is found in *One Hundred Poems From The Japanese*, Kenneth Rexroth's versions of these poems.

"La Catrina" Calavera Catrina, a character originated by the late nineteenth century Mexican illustrator Posada, mocks death with her fine clothes and sauciness.

"Burning" is dedicated to Cal Bedient.

"How Am I Driving?": Big Daddy's voice dominates Tennessee Williams's "Cat on a Hot Tin Roof."

"Mood Sonnet #10": The second line is Colette's. Olympia appears in the eponymous painting by Manet. The third line from the bottom is spoken by Katherine Hepburn in the film "Stage Door" as she rehearses these lines (badly) for her theatrical debut.

The epigraph to Part II is from *Orlando*.

"Love in the Tenth Century": Among this poem's sources are *The World of the Shining Prince: Court Life in Ancient Japan* by Ivan Morris; *The Ink Dark Moon: Love Poems by Ono No Komachi and Izumi Shikibu, Women of the Ancient Court of Japan*, translated by Jane Hirshfield with Mariko Aratani; and Murasaki Shikabu's *The Tale of Genji*.

"Tears": *Yoshiwara: The Glittering World of the Japanese Courtesan* by Cecelia Segawa Seigle is the source of this poem. Edo is the old word for Tokyo; the Yoshiwara was the town's pleasure district.

"Accoutréments": This poem was inspired by *Mirror Images: Women, Surrealism, and Self-Representation,* edited by Whitney Chadwick, which depicts the struggle of female artists in the Surrealist Movement to portray women as subjects and agents.

Mood Sonnet #15": Koko the gorilla is trained to use sign language with which she communicates her many thoughts and feelings.

"Mood Sonnet #19": The film alluded to is Werner Herzog's "Nosferatu."

"Mood Sonnet #20": Izumi Shikabu was one of the great court poets of the Heian Era.